Introduction

This guide covers the area running eastward from the coast around Oban to the stretch of the A82 between Tyndrum and the Black Mount. The area's western boundary is made up of four islands – Lismore, Kerrera, Seil and Luing. To the north and east it is enclosed by the border of Argyll and Bute, while the southern boundary follows a line from Kilmelford to Tyndrum, slicing Loch Awe in half.

The area is well described in the romantic Victorian prose of the 1882 Ordnance Gazetteer.

"The shore is sandy, broken with islands and indentations; the coast behind is generally high, but not rocky, embellished with woods and mansions. The interior ranges from undulating meadow along the coast to high mountain on the farther watershed, or rises away in a great variety of height and contour and terminates in alpine masses,

cleft by deep glens and striped with torrents or cataracts. The scenery everywhere is richly diversified and strikingly picturesque."

The walks described here pass over the undulating meadows of Lismore (*10,11*), the alpine masses of Ben Cruachan (*23*) and Beinn Dòrain (*2*) and the deep cleft of Glen Ure (*6*). There are also torrents, cataracts, forests, castles and, if you are lucky, deer, seals, otters and eagles.

The principal geographical features in the area – Loch Linnhe, Glen Orchy, Loch Awe and most of the major lochs and glens – run south-west to north-east. There are exceptions: Loch Creran and Loch Etive both cut eastwards from the Lynn of Lorn, though even they swing to the north-east as they enter the mountains.

Seil Bridge: 'The bridge over the Atlantic'

The beautiful Ben Cruachan, rising steeply from the shores of Loch Awe, is the dominant mountain in the area, and can be seen from many of the walks. 'Cruachan' means simply 'heaps' or 'stacks' (presumably a reference to its line of pointed peaks), but the name was adopted as a war cry by Clan Campbell, the most powerful clan in this part of the Highlands.

The bulk of the area is formed of granite and other igneous rocks, but amongst the mountains and rugged crags there are also bands of limestone. Here, the landscape changes radically. The green island of Lismore (*10,11*) could be part of the Yorkshire Dales, and Glen Stockdale (*7*) has over thirty caves, including the deepest in Scotland.

Inevitably, in a land where there is so much rock and so little farmland, quarrying has played an important economic role. Granite is still quarried at Bonawe (*13*), while limestone was quarried on Lismore, where the old lime kilns can still be seen.

But it was roofing slate which provided the greatest industry. The derelict quarries on Luing and Seil (*20, 21*) and the adjacent island of Easdale, serviced the building boom of the industrial revolution. There was an iron foundry in Bonawe (*22*), but it was based not on local iron ore but on the forests of Glen Etive and Glen Nant (*24*), which supplied the charcoal required for the smelting process.

In the past, this area was much more populous and politically important than it is today. In the short stretch of coastline that makes up the western boundary there are no less than nine castles, two cathedrals (and the site of a third) and two priories, plus many sacred sites and tales of battles and raids. The last great Viking fleet to invade Britain assembled in the quiet Horseshoe Bay on Kerrera (*18*).

Loch Linnhe was one of the busy highways of medieval Scotland; part of the Great Glen, along which goods and people travelled from coast to coast. The island of Lismore, strategically sited in the middle of the loch, was an important military and religious centre. St Columba originally intended to set up his mission here, but was beaten to the site by St Moluag and had to go to Iona instead. St Moluag died in 592, but there was a cathedral on Lismore until the eighteenth century (*10*).

Inland, as well as the endless skirmishes over clan territory and stolen cattle, there were major military campaigns. Robert the Bruce fought his way through the Pass of Brander (*23*) in 1308, while Montrose later led his army through Glen Creran (*4*) on the way to his victory at Inverlochy (1645).

In the Jacobite rebellion of 1745, the bulk of this area stood for the Hanoverians. The Appin Stewarts, however, were Jacobites and paid the price of defeat. The caves of Glen Stockdale made dismal hiding places for their dispossessed leaders.

The main town in the area is Oban, built around a deep bay with its entrance sheltered by the island of Kerrera (*18*). It is a busy port and a major ferry terminus for the Western Isles.

Driving directions to the starts of the walks are generally given from Oban. There are three main roads: the A816 running south to Lochgilphead; the A85 running north then east to join the A82 Glasgow road at Tyndrum; and the A828 leading north to Fort William.

This is a beautiful area. Enjoy your walking!

Oban: MacCaig's Tower & the Distillery

1 Bridge of Orchy to Tyndrum ─────B

An easy section of the West Highland Way, linking two villages, following a good track. Food and drink are available at both ends of the route.
Length: 6 miles/9.5km (one way); **Height Climbed: 200ft/60m**. *It is possible to walk one way and return by bus or train.*

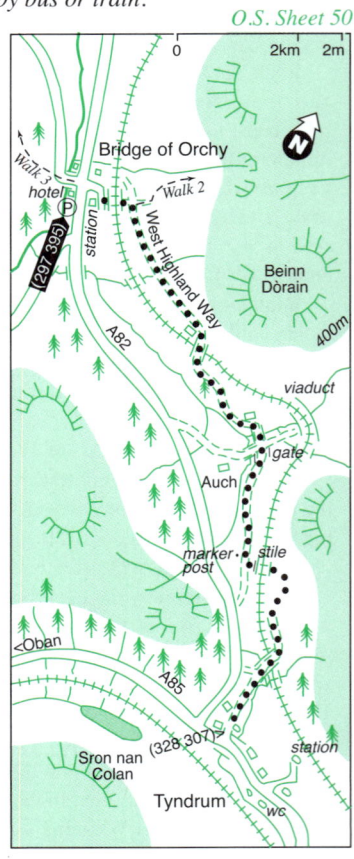

O.S. Sheet 50

The West Highland Way (WHW) runs 96 miles/154km from Glasgow to Fort William. A short section of the route passes through the eastern end of this area (*see also* Walk 3).

Start from Bridge of Orchy, 6 miles north of Tyndrum on the A82 (alternatively, you can park at Tyndrum, take the train or bus to the other end of the route and walk back). Park in the car park by the hotel and walk up to the station. Go under the railway and turn right, following the marked track beneath the slopes of Beinn Dòrain (Walk 2).

This track, originally a military road, was the main Glasgow to Fort William road until the 1930s.

The track runs above the railway for a little over a mile/1.6km, then crosses it and continues, descending to cross a bridge over a river by the farm at Auch (note the railway viaduct up to the left). Beyond the bridge there is a four-way junction. Keep straight on here; climbing with the railway to the left and the river to the right. After a mile/1.6km watch for a WHW marker to the right of the track. At this point leave the track and cut left beneath the railway (NB: if you reach the main road, you have missed the turn).

Continue above the railway line, joining a track after a short distance. This crosses the railway and descends to Tyndrum.

2 Beinn Dòrain _____ A+

The western and southern slopes of Beinn Dòrain look positively intimidating, but the ascent up Coire an Dòthaidh is straightforward and the view from the summit is exhilarating. Length: **5 miles/8km** (there and back); *Height Climbed:* **2900ft/885m**.

O.S. Sheet 50

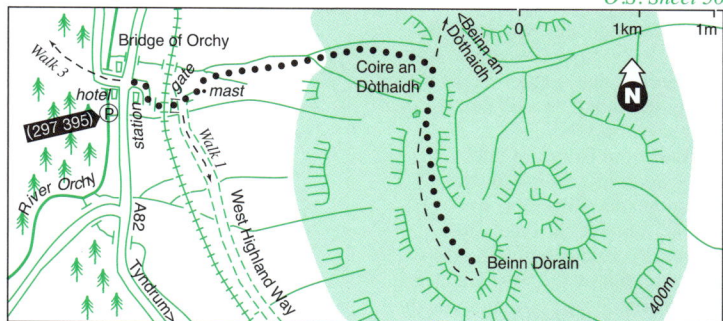

Beinn Dòrain is the steep, smooth-sided hill which rises dramatically to the east of Glen Orchy. Start from the car park adjacent to the Bridge of Orchy Hotel, 6 miles north of Tyndrum on the A82 Glasgow to Fort William road. Cross the road (take care, it can be busy) and walk up the road to the station (you are asked not to park here). Go under the railway line and follow the path (part of the West Highland Way) up steps to a metal gate which leads onto a broad, clear track.

Cross this track and take the clear track beyond, leading up to a telephone mast. Just before the mast, cut left onto a small, clear path. Follow this to the head of Coire an Dòthaidh. Turn right on the watershed and either follow the ridge to the summit or take the clear path which runs along the west slope of the hill before doubling back to the top.

From here you can look down on the curve of the railway line and the road far below. To the west are the mountains of Glen Etive; to the east the hills around Glen Lyon.

Descend the same way. The summit of Beinn an Dòthaidh (also a Munro) is not far from the head of the coire, to the north, and is well worth the extra mile.

Beinn Dòrain (on the right) and Beinn an Dòthaidh, seen from the west (see Walk 3)

3 Bridge of Orchy to Inveroran ————————————B

This is a circular walk from Bridge of Orchy, starting along part of the West Highland Way and returning along a quiet single-track road. The Inveroran Hotel, once a famous drovers' inn, is at the halfway point.
Length: **5¹/₃ miles/8.5km**; *Height Climbed:* **530ft/160m**.

O.S. Sheet 50

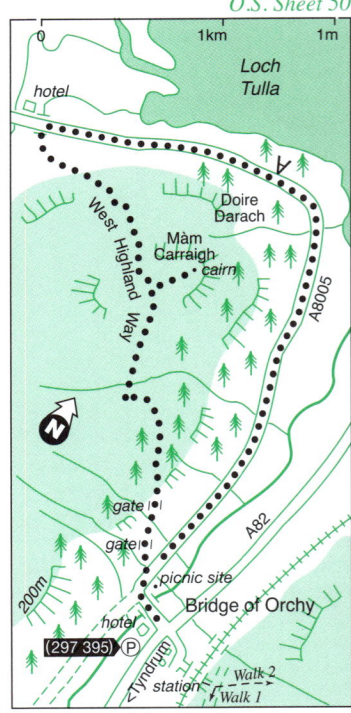

The West Highland Way runs 96 miles/154km from Glasgow to Fort William. A short section of the path passes through the eastern end of this area (*see also* Walk 1).

Start from Bridge of Orchy, 6 miles north of Tyndrum on the A82. Cross the old bridge over the river (A8005), beside the hotel. Just beyond the bridge turn left, off the road, and follow the West Highland Way marker posts; passing through two gates and a conifer wood. The path climbs steadily, clearing the trees to reach a watershed. (At this point, a short diversion to the right leads to the cairn on the summit of Màm Carraigh. From here there are fine views of Loch Tulla and of the superb mountain backdrop beyond.)

Descend to the road at the Inveroran Hotel, near the head of Loch Tulla. The West Highland Way continues to the left, but for this route turn right and follow the single track road back to Bridge of Orchy, along the shores of the loch and through the Doire Darach pine forest.

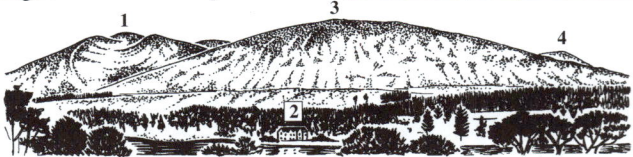

1 *Stob Ghabhar (1087m)* **2** *Black Mount* **3** *Beinn Toaig (834m)* **4** *Creag an Fhirich (700m)*

4 Glen Creran to Ballachulish _____ A

A lineal walk between two glens. The path climbs through forest to a watershed then descends through moorland to Ballachulish. Length: **7 miles/11km** *(one way); Height Climbed:* **1200ft/370m**. *A bus service links Ballachulish and Creagan Bridge: add* 4 miles/6km *to the route for the walk from the bridge to Elleric car park.*

O.S. Sheets 41 & 50

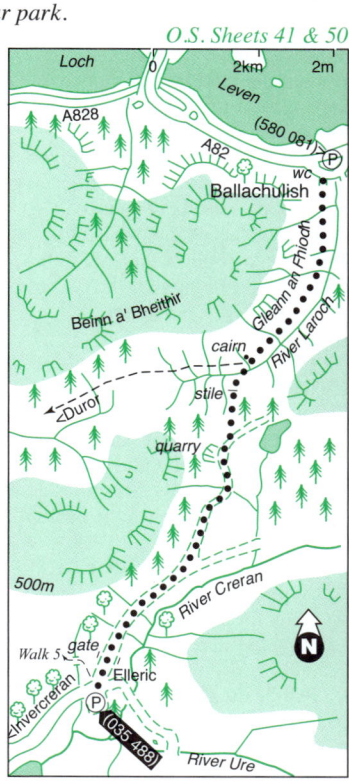

Start from the car park at Elleric, at the end of the Invercreran road. To reach it, drive 14 miles north of Oban on the A828 Fort William road to Creagan Bridge (crossing Loch Creran). On the far side, take the second exit at the roundabout, signposted for Invercreran. Where the road turns over a bridge at the head of the loch, keep straight on up the road which ends at Elleric.

From the car park, follow the forestry track (green post with footprint) through mixed woodland for 1 mile/1.6km to a fork. Take the left-hand track, which climbs with fine views of Beinn Fhionnlaidh and Beinn Sgulaird (*see* Walk 6).

After approximately 3½ miles/ 5km, there is a sign to the left (ROW to Ballachulish). Follow this path, which climbs steeply at first through larch trees, then zig-zags across open ground to reach a stile at the bealach. Two parallel paths are visible on the far side of the River Laroch below.

Cross the stile and follow a steep, indistinct path down into Gleann an Fhiodh. On the far side of the glen you will see an obvious cairn with a sign beside it. Cross the River Laroch to reach the cairn, then turn right, down the glen. (A turn to the left here leads to Duror: *see* OS map for details of this route).

The path gradually becomes clearer as it nears Ballachulish.

5 Two Short Walks in Glen Creran ———————— C

A) *A short, steep waymarked circular walk through ancient woodland on the side of Loch Creran. Length:* **¾ mile/1km**; *Height Climbed:* **300ft/100m**. **B)** *A short waymarked Forestry Commission walk with great views of surrounding hills. Length:* **1¼ miles/2km**; *Height Climbed:* **300ft/100m**.

O.S. Sheet 49 & 50

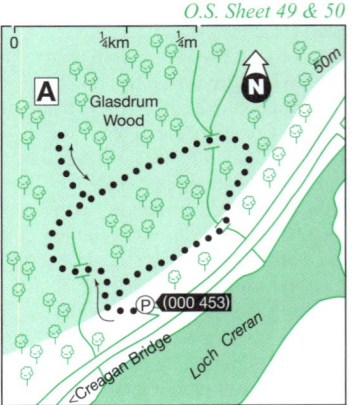

Walk A) This walk starts from the car park for Glasdrum National Nature Reserve. To reach it, drive 14 miles north from Oban on the A828 Fort William road to Creagan Bridge (crossing Loch Creran). On the far side, take the second exit at the roundabout, signposted for Invercreran. Follow this for 2 miles, and look for the sign for the car park on your left, just before the end of the loch.

The walk leaves the car park and climbs, through pleasant oak woodland, above the loch. At the junction, keep left and follow the circuit in a clockwise direction.

O.S. Sheet 50

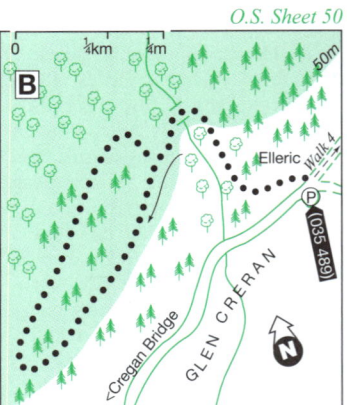

Walk B) Follow the directions given in Walk 4 to reach the Forestry Commission car park at Elleric.

Walk out of the car park on a forest road signposted to Salachail, and look for an interpretive panel marking the start of the path to the left after a few metres.

Follow the clear waymarked path as it climbs through woodland to a bridge over a burn. After a short distance you reach a junction. Keep straight on to follow the circuit in a clockwise direction.

The views of the surrounding hills from cleared sections are superb.

6 Around Beinn Sgulaird — A+

A circular walk through spectacular mountain scenery and the dramatic cleft of Glen Ure. Length: **14 miles/23km**; *Height Climbed:* **1800ft/ 550m**. *Burn crossings may be difficult after heavy rain.*

O.S. Sheet 50

NB: *New tracks and fences are being put in on this section. Some navigation may be required.*

Drive 13 miles north of Oban on the A828 and turn left on the minor road off the roundabout before the Creagan Bridge. The road passes a large white house. Park just beyond, in a lay-by to the right of the road.

Walk back towards Oban for a few metres and turn off first left, through a kissing gate beside a metal gate (Druimavuic). Follow a clear track uphill through scattered trees, pass through a gate (Ben Sgulaird), and continue on the track up the glen of Allt Buidhe, ignoring paths off to the right. Near the top of the climb the track deteriorates, but it is never in doubt. After 3 miles/5km you reach the pass at the top of the corrie.

A rough, intermittent path descends steeply on the far side, winding down to a crossing point on a burn (056 435) below the slopes of Beinn Mheadonach.

After crossing the burn, turn left. The faint path climbs to a watershed at the head of the burn then descends towards Glen Ure, becoming less clear. (If in doubt, aim towards the left-hand edge of a conifer wood visible on a slope ahead.)

Ford the river just below a stream junction (080 464 – cross higher up if the river is in spate). After the ford, the path climbs briefly then descends to cross a burn between two lochans. Beyond the burn, join a good track which leads back over the river then down the gorge of upper Glen Ure.

Continue down the glen. In a stand of fine Scots pine, a track heads back right. Ignore this and go straight on, through a kissing gate. Beyond this, keep to the main track, ignoring tracks to left and right. Continue down Glen Creran, with the river on your right, to reach the public road.

7 Glen Stockdale _____A

A rewarding linear walk, on mixed paths, up a fine glen. Most people will walk part of the route, there-and-back, but it is possible to continue on forest roads to reach the public road and return by the coastal cycle track. **Length: 7 miles/11km** (through route), **13 miles/21km** (full circuit); **Height Climbed: 825ft/250m**.

O.S. Sheet 49

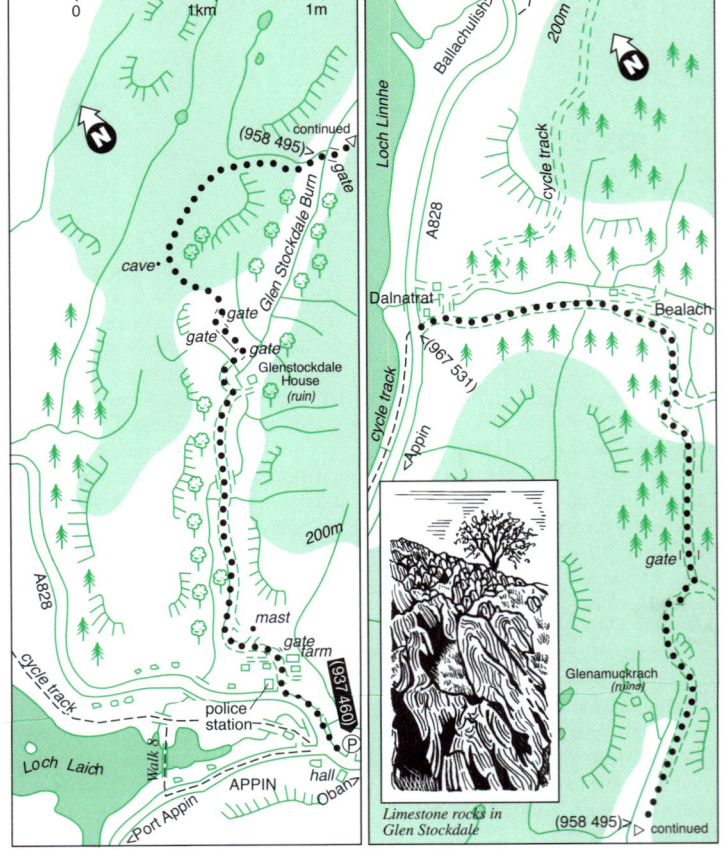

Limestone rocks in Glen Stockdale

Park in the car park opposite Appin Village Hall, 15 miles north of Oban on the A828, just before the turn-off for Port Appin. Walk north by the road (taking great care), past the junction and on to the police station, a short distance beyond. At this point turn right and follow a quiet road up to the buildings at Kinlochlaich Farm. Go left, through a gate. There is now a house in front of you. Go hard right, through a second gate, and follow a clear, rough track up the glen.

After the track crosses a bridge over the burn, the glen opens up. As the track approaches the low ruin of Glenstockdale House it splits. Keep left (the right-hand track fords the river to reach the ruin).

Beyond the split, follow the route marked by the arrows to reach a gate. Go through the gate and turn left, up the left-hand side of a steep field, to reach an old gate in the top corner of the field. Go through this, and the gap in the old wall beyond. Follow the wall for 70m to reach an ash tree where a stream goes underground. Beyond this, continue along a rough path for a short distance to reach a gate in a new fence. Go through this and continue along a faint path, climbing gently to reach the top of a low limestone ridge with exposed, jagged rows of rocks along it.

If you make a short detour to your left, at this point, you should see a small marshy burn dropping into the entrance to a cave. This was one of the hiding places of Charles Stewart of Ardsheal (who led the Stewarts of Appin during the '45 rising) in the aftermath of the Battle of Culloden.

Note the fine view down the Lynn of Lorn then continue along the ridge, using the sharp blades of limestone as a guide. When it runs down into marshy ground (after about 500m) follow a sheep track just above the tree and bracken line (to the right of the marsh) until the limestone and the ridge re-emerge. Stay on the ridge as it descends to the main Glenstockdale Burn at a stream junction (958 495).

On the far side of the burn is a metal field gate. Ford the burn and go through this to join a rough track. Follow this up the glen. Though the track is indistinct in places, there is no doubt about the route, climbing towards the watershed and passing the ruins at Glenamuckrach on the far side of the glen.

Beyond the watershed, the track descends to reach a junction with a clearer track. A short detour to the right at this point leads to a small loch, but to complete the circuit go left, quickly reaching a gate. Go through this.

From here it is two miles/3km dropping down on forest roads to reach the cycle track just before the public road. Navigation is simple: just keep left at the two remaining junctions. To complete the circuit, cross the A828 (carefully) and turn left along the cycle track. It is a pleasant 6 mile/9km walk along the coast back to the start.

8 Jubilee Bridge — C

A short lineal walk over a bridge across mud flats and salt marsh, leading to a cycle track by the shore. Fine views of Castle Stalker. **Length: 3 miles/5km** (there and back); *Height Climbed:* none.

O.S. Sheet 49

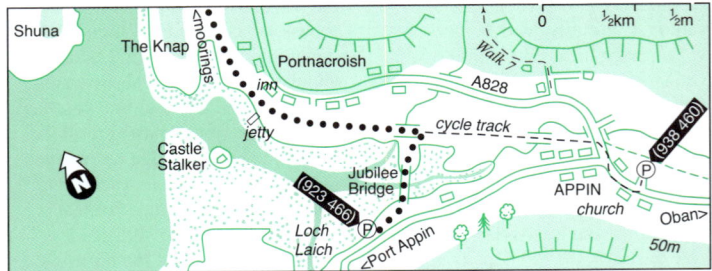

About 15 miles north of Oban on the A828, turn west at the signpost for Port Appin and the Lismore Ferry. The small car park for the Jubilee Bridge is on the right after one mile. (**NB:** If this is full, there is a larger car park in the village. To join the walk from here, follow the pavement by the A828 to reach the cycle track, then turn left.)

From the small car park, the tarred path (now a link to the Oban/Fort William cycle track), leads past a bird hide and over the mud flats to the bridge, with fine views of Castle Stalker sitting on its rock in the middle of the loch. A series of interpretive panels along the path tell you about the bridge, the castle and the mud flats.

Walk across the long, low, wooden bridge, which was totally refurbished in 2014. (At low tide the burn and the area of salt marsh surrounding it are a great place to view wading birds.) Beyond the bridge, continue on the boardwalk and tarred path, eventually climbing to join the cycle track, which follows the line of the old Oban to Ballachulish railway.

Turn left along the track. In a little under a mile/1.6km you reach the jetty for Castle Stalker (open to visitors, booking essential: **www.castlestalker.com**). Continue along the cycle track for a further 1/2 mile/0.8km to reach the moorings at Lettershuna, from where there are views across to the little island of Shuna. Retrace your steps to return to the start.

Castle Stalker

9 Clach Thoull ─────────────────────── C

A short, easily followed circular walk round Clach Thoull ('The Holed Rock'). This is a sea-arch that was formed by wave action when the sea level was several metres higher than it is today. Length: **1½ miles/ 2.4km**; *Height Climbed:* none.

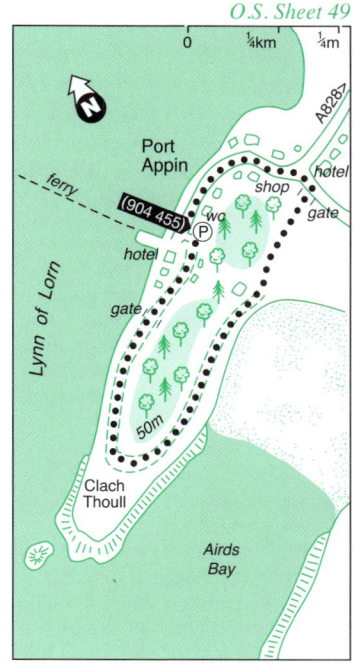

O.S. Sheet 49

Drive about 14 miles north of Oban on the A828 and turn west at the signpost for Port Appin and the Lismore Ferry. Follow this road to its conclusion at the pier in Port Appin. The walk starts from the car park and is signposted.

A well-made track runs behind the Pier House Hotel and along the raised beach behind the coast. To your left is the vast, pale quartzite block, covered with mixed vegetation and ringed by cliffs, which is one of the chief attractions of this walk. There are also good views out to Lismore and to Ben More on Mull. When you reach the end of the headland it is possible to walk through the arch and to look into the shallow caves – worn out of the cliffs by ancient wave action.

The path continues around the headland along Airds Bay, beneath the ancient sea cliffs. The large white house at the head of the bay is the 18th-century Airds House. The distinctive peak in the distance is Ben a' Bheither.

Go round the front of a white house and follow the path signed for Port Appin into the trees. When this emerges onto a single-track road turn left, past the Airds Hotel and the shop, to return to the car park.

Clach Thoull

10 The Broch of Tirefour & Castle Coeffin /
11 Achnacroish to Achadun Castle & Sailean___B/B

Two circular walks on the island of Lismore. The first is described from the Port Appin ferry, although it can be walked from Achnacroish. The second starts from Achnacroish. Much of the walking is on quiet, single-track roads. **10)** *A Pictish broch, a spectacular ruined castle and stunning scenery. Length:* **9 miles/15km**; *Height Climbed:* **250ft/75m**.
11) *A circular walk that takes you along a beautiful and desolate coastline, with an out and back spur to the ruins of a 13th-century castle. Length:* **8½ miles/11km** (**4½ miles/7km** for just the Sailean circuit); *Height Climbed:* **300ft/90m**.

O.S. Sheet 49

Lismore is a beautiful limestone island in the middle of Loch Linnhe. The landscape and flora are in striking contrast to the heather-covered granite hills of the mainland. You can reach the island by pedestrian ferry from Port Appin (Walk 9) (10 minutes), or by car ferry from Oban to Achnacroish (50 minutes). Contact Oban Visitor Information Centre for times, or look at www.isleoflismore.com.

Walk 10) Take the passenger ferry from Port Appin. From the ferry landing, follow the road south. After about 2 miles/3km turn off left at a signpost for the broch (fort) and follow the road until you reach a gate to the left marked by a sign for Achnacroish and the broch.

Climb easily to the broch then go right (south) along the low ridge. Go through a gate in a fence. Shortly beyond this, the faint path joins a fence to your left, with trees and a cliff beyond. Continue to reach a metal ladder stile over a stone dyke.

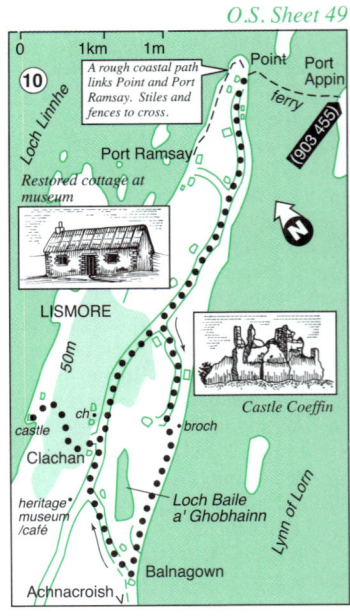

Cross this and continue to reach a further dyke. Cut left here, down a shallow gully, to reach a gate in a dyke. You are now on the raised beach. Continue along this to reach the white cottage at Balnagown. (There is a good path along the shore from here to Achnacroish.)

Turn right just before the cottage and follow the track up to a farm. Go through the gate to join the public road and follow this past Loch Baile a' Ghobhainn to reach the main road along the centre of the island.

Turn right along this for 800m to reach the houses at Clachan. Just beyond the first house to the left (a farmhouse with outbuildings), turn left and follow a clear track through a field. Beyond a gate, turn left onto a rougher track, which leads down to the dramatic ruin of Castle Coeffin by a small bay.

Return to Clachan and continue along the road to reach the ferry. It is worth stopping off at the church, built on the site of a cathedral founded by St Moluag in the 6th century. Half a mile from Clachan, on your left, you will see Moluag's Chair: a chair-shaped stone.

Walk 11) From the ferry pier at Achnacroish, follow the road uphill to join the main road and turn left (Achinduin). After about 500m keep right at a junction. In a little under a mile/1.6km you will pass the start of a signposted track to Sailean on your right.

If you're going to the castle, keep straight on. The road ends at a group of houses. The track splits: keep left. At the next junction keep right (arrow). Pass a marshy area to your left and go through a gate.

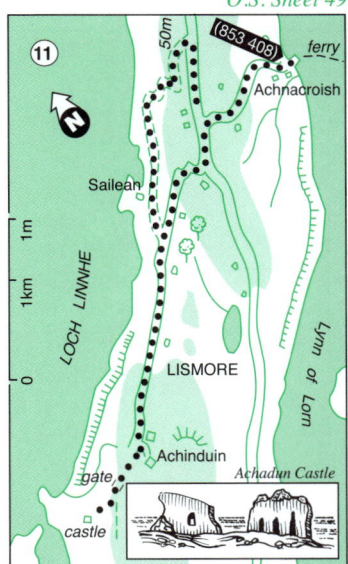

O.S. Sheet 49

When you see a fence coming in from the left ahead, turn right onto a fainter, grassy path. Achadun Castle – once the seat of the Bishops of Argyll – quickly becomes visible below. Follow the rough path down to the castle then return by the same route to the Salean junction.

For the Salean circuit, turn onto the clear track, climbing then descending to the sea. Follow the track north along the coast (it may be covered at high tide), noting the old lime kilns and empty cottages. After a mile/1.6km the track turns inland and leads over the hill to the main road. Turn right to return to Achnacroish.

Walks Oban & North Argyll

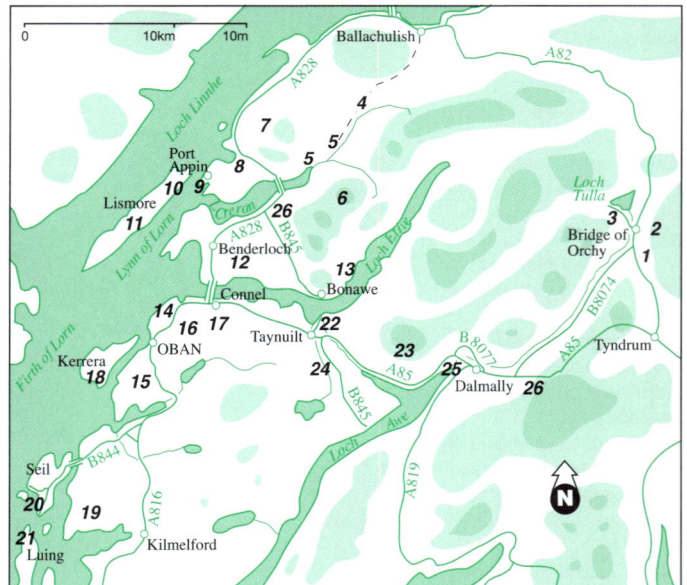

Grades

A+ ... Full walking equipment – including map and compass – and previous hill walking experience essential

A ...... Full walking equipment required

B ...... Strong walking footwear and waterproof clothing required

C ...... Comfortable walking footwear recommended

NB: Assume each walk increases at least one grade in winter conditions, **A** and **A+** routes becoming extremely treacherous.

www.pocketwalks.com

Published by: *Hallewell Publications, Scotland*
Printed by: *Barr Printers, Glenrothes*

While every care has been taken in the preparation of this guide, the publishers cannot accept responsibility for any loss, damage or injury resulting from its use.

Walks Oban & North Argyll

walk		grade
1	Bridge of Orchy to Tyndrum	B
2	Beinn Dòrain	A+
3	Bridge of Orchy to Inveroran	B
4	Glen Creran to Ballachulish	A
5	Two Short Walks in Glen Creran	C
6	Around Beinn Sgulaird	A+
7	Glen Stockdale	A
8	Jubilee Bridge	C
9	Clach Thoull	C
10	The Broch of Tirefour & Castle Coeffin	B
11	Achnacroish to Achadun Castle & Sailean	B
12	Beinn Lora	B
13	Eilean Uisneachan	B
14	Ganavan to Dunstaffnage	B
15	Oban to Gallanach	B
16	The Old Coach Road	B
17	The Black Lochs	B
18	Kerrera	B
19	Bealach Gaoithe & The Wishing Tree	B
20	Ellanbeich to Cuan	B
21	Luing Quarries	B
22	Bonawe Furnace & The River Awe	B
23	Ben Cruachan	A+
24	Glen Nant Oakwoods	C
25	Kilchurn Castle	C
26	Two Forest Walks	C

12 Beinn Lora — B

A modest hill climb, mostly on well-made waymarked paths (steep in places), but the last half mile/0.9km is on the open hillside and can be muddy, wet and windy. Splendid views. Length: up to 3¾ miles/6km *(there and back); Height Climbed:* **1020ft/308m**.

O.S. Sheet 49

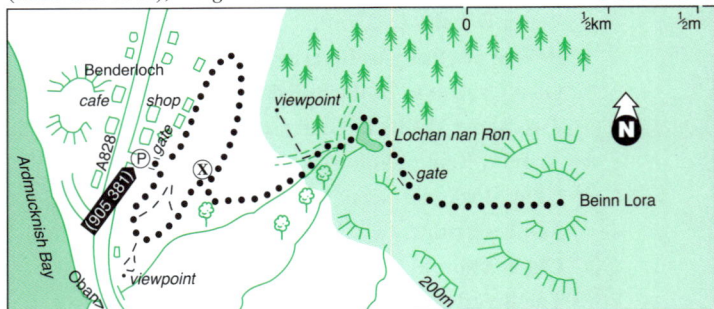

This is a steep walk, but it provides terrific coastal views. These can be enjoyed from the numerous seats and benches along the route.

To reach the walk, drive 7 miles north of Oban on the A828 Fort William road. Just as you enter the village of Benderloch there is a Forestry Commission car park to the right of the road. There is map (and a leaflet dispenser) in the car park showing two possible routes (*see* map) – the climb to the summit and a steep circuit on the lower slopes.

For both walks, walk out of the back of the car park on a clear path (blue/red), going round a gate. When the path splits, just beyond, go right.

The clear path climbs steeply, parallel to the coast, with fine views over Ardmucknish Bay and out to the islands. Continue climbing, ignoring paths cutting off to the left and right, to reach a junction (**X**). For the circuit, go left (blue/red). To complete the climb, go right (blue).

On the blue route, the path climbs steeply to reach a forest road. To reach the Eagle's Eyrie viewpoint, go left then almost immediately right (marker). To reach the summit of Beinn Lora, go right, continuing uphill on the forest road.

You reach a forest road junction. Cross this and follow the path directly opposite, passing the reed-filled Lochan nan Ron, then climbing to reach the edge of the forest, where there is a gate onto the open hillside.

The muddy but well-trodden path descends, then zig-zags up to the round trig point on the summit.

Enjoy the views, then retrace your steps to junction (**X**). Keep straight on here, following the clear path back to the car park (blue/red).

13 Eilean Uisneachan   B

This linear walk has a somewhat inauspicious start through the Bonawe quarry workings, but these are quickly left behind and it follows an easy track along one of the most beautiful Highland lochs. **Length: 8 miles/13km** (there and back); **Height Climbed: 100ft/30m**. *O.S. Sheet 50*

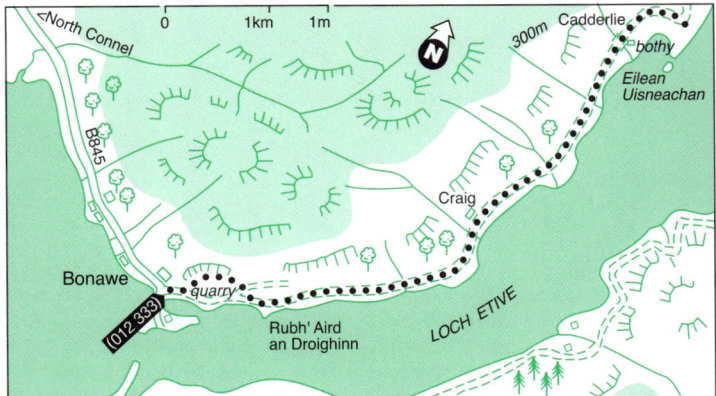

Eilean Uisneachan ('Island of the Uisneachs') was the home of the sons of Uisneach and the beautiful Deirdre of the Sorrows, players in one of the epic Celtic tales of love, jealousy, betrayal and murder.

Drive north from Oban on the A828 Fort William road. Cross the Connel Bridge then go right (North Connel). Continue for 8 miles along Loch Etive. There is room to park by the side of the road just beyond the entrance road to Bonawe quarry.

Follow the sign for the footpath to Glen Etive, down the entrance road. As you approach the quarry workings, go left on a signposted footpath that starts behind the busy quarry and eventually reaches a track running by the loch. Go left, through quarry workings at first, then continue along the track by the loch, passing Rubh' Aird an Droighinn, where Deirdre waved farewell to her lover as he sailed to his death in Ireland.

Continue through mixed woodland to reach Eilean Uisneachan, just beyond the ruins of Cadderlie. This is a convenient place to turn back.

If you can arrange transport, you could continue to the public road at the head of the loch. Alternatively, you could make the complete circuit of the loch, finishing at Taynuilt, opposite Bonawe (24 miles/39km, and possibly a two-day trip). These are serious walks and should not be undertaken lightly.

14 Ganavan to Dunstaffnage ─────────── B

A short linear walk with stunning coastal views, starting from a sandy beach and leading to Dunstaffnage Castle. Length: **3 miles/5km** *(there and back); Height Climbed:* **200ft/60m**.

O.S. Sheet 49

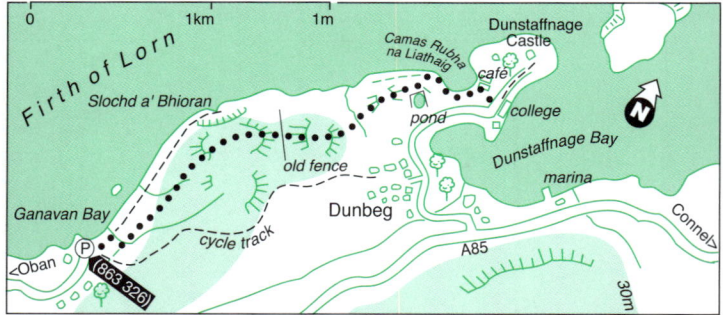

To reach Ganavan Bay, drive north around the coast from Oban, passing the ruin of Dunollie Castle. The road ends at a large car park by the beach.

Continue walking beyond the car park, on a clear path behind the shore. The path passes through a metal kissing-gate. Shortly beyond, it reaches a small burn.

Immediately before the burn the path splits. For a possible short detour, carry straight on on the path below the cliffs. The path narrows and soon reaches a dangerous cleft in the cliff at Slochd a' Bhioran (sharp cleft). The cleft is narrow but deep, and it is best to turn back here.

For the main route, turn right, with the burn to your left. At the top of the first rise there is a four-way junction. Go left, climbing through whin bushes then continuing along a broad, grassy path running parallel to the coast. Follow this over a hilltop (ignoring other paths). It descends to cross an old fence, then continues over the double-peaked hill beyond. Cross a stream beyond this and continue over a further small hill to reach a fence around a pond.

At the far left-hand corner of the fence the path splits. Keep left, heading towards the coast. The path reaches the foot of a low cliff.

Head right along the path beneath the cliff. After a short distance you reach the corner of a fence by the end of the cliff, just behind the rocky shore. Cross the fence and follow the path down to the exquisite bay of Camas Rubha na Liathaig.

To visit Dunstaffnage Castle, turn right on the near side of the grey buildings (college and marine resource centre) on the far side of the bay to join the road. Turn left and walk a few hundred metres. Return by the same route.

15 Oban to Gallanach B

This walk starts from the centre of Oban, climbs to the viewpoint of Pulpit Hill then passes between low hills and descends to the quiet shore of the Sound of Kerrera. Length: **2½ miles/4km** *(one way); Height Climbed:* **250ft/75m**. *Possible link with Walk 18.*

O.S. Sheet 49

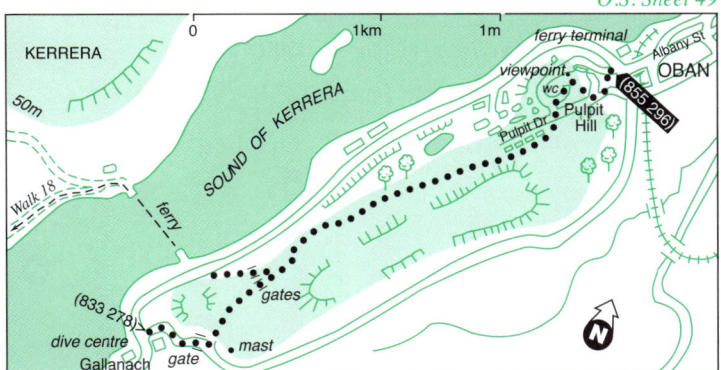

From the centre of Oban, follow the signs for the ferry terminal and Gallanach. Just after crossing the railway, turn left at a sign for Pulpit Hill. At a junction after about 50m follow the sign for the footpath to Pulpit Hill. Go steeply up this path to join the public road. Turn right for about 30m then turn right onto a track with a hedge to the left. At the next junction there is another sign for the footpath. At the end of the path, head up to the viewpoint on the summit. There is a view indicator here, showing all the main features of the splendid view.

Follow the road from the viewpoint. When this reaches a T-junction with another road turn left, then first right onto Pulpit Drive. After 100m there is a sign to the left for the footpath to the Kerrera Ferry. Follow the track, behind houses then on between low hills. The track eventually becomes a muddy path and approaches a fence with two gates in it.

For the ferry (*see* Walk 18), follow the clear path to the right-hand gate then head for a prominent gap in the hills. Go through a gate then follow the obvious track downhill.

Alternatively, go through the left-hand gate then on along the base of the hills. Follow a good path over a low pass to a minor road. Turn right through a gate to reach Gallanach. Either take a bus back to Oban (check times locally) or return by the same route.

16 The Old Coach Road / 17 The Black Lochs — B/B

Two routes between Oban and Connel which can be combined to make a longer circuit. **16)** *An easy linear walk along a quiet, almost derelict track. Length:* **5 miles/8km** *(one way); Height Climbed:* **340ft/102m**. **17)** *A pleasant but complex circular walk which leads from the busy A85 to the quiet landscape of the Black Lochs. Some navigation needed. Length:* **6 miles/9.6km**; *Height Climbed:* **230ft/70m**.

O.S. Sheet 49

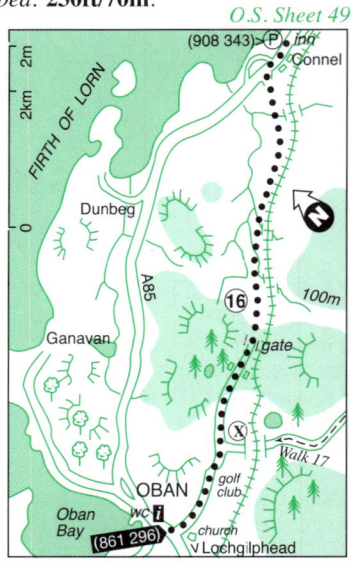

Walk 16) From the centre of Oban walk south along the A816 for Lochgilphead. After about 300m the road forks, with a church in the fork. Keep left (Glencruitten).

Continue along the road, climbing slightly, passing the Glencruitten Golf Club. It is now a single-track road, leaving the houses and winding through trees to reach a fork (**X**). Take the left road, signposted for Achavaich.

The road climbs steadily, and begins to run parallel to the railway before it reaches the old railway houses (The Summit).

Past the houses, the public road ends and a gate opens onto the old road. Follow this for about 2½ miles/4km, until it descends to join the main A85. There are fine views of the hills to the north, Beinn Lora (*see* Walk 12), the Connel narrows and the sweeping curve of Ardmucknish Bay. Turn right and follow the main road (pavement) to The Oyster Inn.

There is a regular bus service from here back into Oban. If you wish to make a circular walk (total distance 13¼ miles/21km) you are now at the start of Walk 17.

Walk 17) Drive 5 miles north of Oban on the A85 and park at the car park and viewpoint for the Falls of Lora (a dramatic tide race beneath the Connel Bridge), opposite The Oyster Inn. Follow the pavement by the main road under the Connel Bridge then on for about ¾ mile/1km, before turning right onto Achaleven Road. Follow the road under the railway and continue until, just after it turns hard left, a track heads off to the right. Turn on to this, passing Achaleven Croft. When the track forks, just beyond, keep left, climbing a slope.

When the track begins to drop towards the houses at Cuil-uaine ('The Green Hollow') the first of the Black Lochs comes into view. Pass through a gate by the first house, beyond which the track splits. Go right, passing behind a white house to your left then following the clear track through a gated farmyard.

Continue on the track to reach a further gate (ignore the track to the left just before it). Beyond this there is a series of junctions. Keep left at all of them and you should find yourself on a clear, damp track contouring across a wooded slope with the higher ground to your right.

The track curves right and reaches a junction, roughly level with the end of the loch, with a clear, stony track heading off to the right. Go left here, off the track, on a faint grassy path which descends then climbs gently to reach an old metal gate. Beyond the gate you are in open grazing land. Bear slightly right to reach a gate in a fence, visible ahead.

Walk half-right across the field beyond (no path) towards a craggy hillside with miniature scree slopes. Walk along the foot of this slope, with a fence to your left, to reach the corner of a stone wall. Continue with the wall to your left to reach a gate level with Kilvaree farm. Go through this and follow the wall

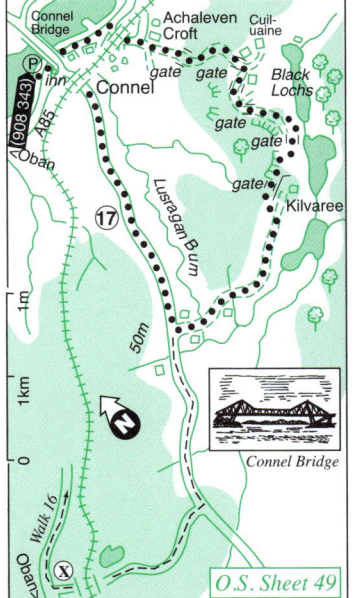

down to join the access track to the farm. Go right.

The track runs along the shore of the reed-choked lower loch, then turns right, over the Lusragan Burn and up to join a single-track road. Turn right here and follow this quiet road for 2 miles/3km back to the main road and your starting point.

If you wish to make a longer circuit, incorporating Walk 16 (total distance 11 miles/18km), turn left and walk for just over a mile/1.6km to a right turn, signposted for Oban. Follow this road for one and a half miles to the Achavaich turn off (**X**). You are now on Walk 16.

18 Kerrera B

There are lots of possible walks on the island of Kerrera and, since it is barely 4 miles by 2 miles, it is hard to get lost! This circular walk is an introduction to this fine island. Length: **7 miles/11km**; *Height Climbed:* **300ft/90m**. *Refreshments are available at the Tea Garden.* O.S. Sheet 49

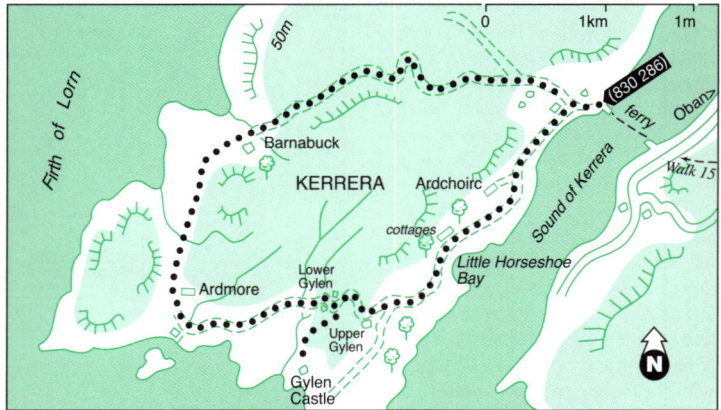

Kerrera is the island which provides the western protection for the splendid natural harbour of Oban Bay. The island is inhabited but the roads are unmetalled and there is no car ferry.

The ferry is just south of Oban. To reach it, look for the sign for Gallanach at the main roundabout and follow a single-track road for 2 miles along the shore. (There is also a bus service, or you could walk out from Oban following Walk 15.) Check ferry times locally.

At the junction above the jetty on Kerrera keep left and follow the track by the coast. At the next junction, keep left again. After passing the cottages at Little Horseshoe Bay the track pulls away from the shore.

Climb to a clear junction. Keep straight on here ('Gylen Castle'), passing the house at Upper Gylen before dropping to Lower Gylen (Tea Garden). Just before the latter, a path on the left leads to the ruin of Gylen Castle – built by the MacDougalls in the 16th century. From the castle, retrace your steps to the track and continue in the original direction.

The track stops just before the house at Ardmore. Continue on a rough path which climbs to the left of the house and runs for a little under a mile/1.6km to the farm at Barnabuck. From here, follow a good track which climbs steeply then descends to return to the ferry.

19 **Bealach Gaoithe & The Wishing Tree** ─────**B**

An excursion across the fascinating Degnish peninsula to the north side of Loch Melfort. There are fine views out over Seil, Luing and the Craignish peninsula. Length: **6 miles/9.5km** *(there and back); Height Climbed:* **350ft/110m**.

O.S. Sheet 55

Start from beside the gates of Ardmaddy Castle, about 12 miles south of Oban. To reach it, follow the A816 Lochgilphead road from Oban for about 8 miles, then turn right on the B844 Easdale road. After about 3 miles, take the single-track road signposted for Ardmaddy.

Where the road turns right through the castle gates, a broad track leads straight ahead ('Degnish'). Park here – space is very limited: please avoid blocking gates and access along tracks. Follow the signposted track, passing through a number of gates and ignoring tracks to right and left before climbing towards the bealach (pass).

Bealach Gaoithe can be loosely translated as 'windy gap', and the winds that funnel through here have toppled the famous Wishing Tree. It now lies in a small enclosure, just below the bealach. There are hundreds of coins hammered into its trunk, some horse shoes jammed in a fork and usually a few ribbons hanging from the branches. Judging by the new coins, the fallen tree still retains its magical powers!

The track runs on through open grassland and moorland before descending to reach the end of the public road along Loch Melfort near the farm at Degnish. Return the same way.

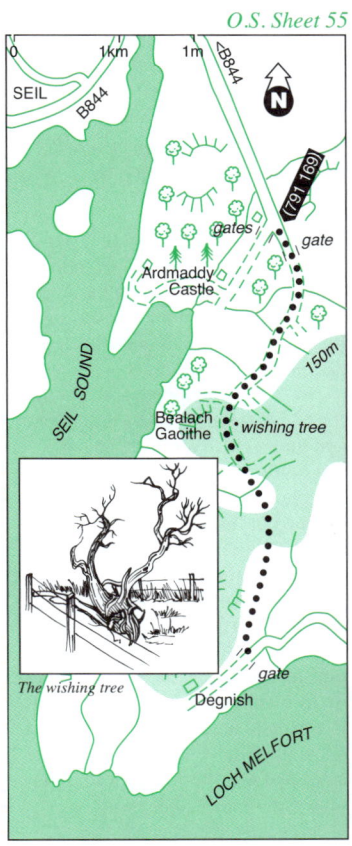

The wishing tree

20 **Ellanbeich to Cuan** / 21 **Luing Quarries** — **B/B**

Luing, Seil and the nearby island of Easdale were once the home to a thriving slate industry, and the old quarry workings and grassed-over tracks add a poignancy to the spectacular coastal scenery. The latter includes views of Scarba, the Garvellachs and the hills of Jura.

Seil is linked to the mainland by the famous – and actually very short – 'Bridge over the Atlantic', while a five minute ferry crossing from Seil takes you to Luing. **Walk 20)** *A linear walk on Seil. Length:* **3 miles/4.5km** *(one way); Height Climbed:* **none**. **Walk 21)** *A circular walk past the old quarry workings on Luing. Length:* **4 miles/6.5km**; *Height Climbed:* **160ft/50m**. *Part of this walk is not possible at full high tide.*

O.S. Sheet 55

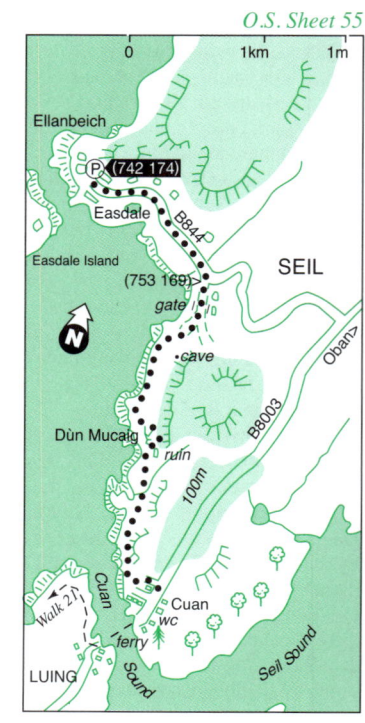

Walk 20) Ellanbeich, on the island of Seil, is about 15 miles from Oban. To reach it, head south on the A816 Lochgilphead road and follow signs for Seil and then Easdale. There is car parking in the village.

Walk back along the road (busy at times) for a little under a mile/1.6km and turn right at a row of houses, just before the road leaves the shore and climbs steeply uphill. Go along the road in front of the houses and through a metal gate then follow the track along the coast.

Continue on the track, and pass through a gate. Beyond this, just stick by the coast (the path is indistinct in places). You go round a rocky headland, beyond which there is a marshy area to your left with an arena of cliffs beyond. Stick by the coast and pass through a wall in a section of natural dyke.

Scramble across stones behind the shore to reach the next headland, beyond which is a big detached mass of rock called Dùn Mucaig. For the best view, go through the gap between Dùn Mucaig and the cliff, then turn right, past an old ruin, to rejoin the path at the coast.

Cross a ladder stile over a fence (visible from the ruin) and turn left. After a few paces there is a second stile to your left. Cross this and continue, with the fence to your right at first, then continue along the shore until you join the end of a track leading to the public road. Turn right and follow the road to Cuan.

NB: If you are starting this walk from Cuan, take the *second* turn to the left as you climb from the ferry to join the track leading to the shore.

Walk 21) Take the track on the right at the ferry waiting room and follow it round the coast. Pass through a gate by a small harbour, and continue on the rough path beyond. There are many signs of the old workings: small quarries and slate heaps. The path goes around Cuan Point, then past the inlet of Port Mary. Here the track forks, but follow the coast. Cross a natural dyke by a stile close to the cliffs and then return to the shore.

If you feel energetic, it's worth following a path up the grassy slope, through piles of slate and past a small quarry, to the top of the cliffs. There are fine views, but be careful – the cliff is high, steep and windy! If you make this diversion, return the way you came and continue round the base of the cliffs. If you go along the cliff top, you'll find yourself up above Cullipool with no way down.

The first part of the track round the shore has been washed away so go very carefully over the rocks, then climb up on to the path for an easy, level walk to Cullipool past the big quarry workings in the sea cliffs.

Follow the road along the shore through the village, past the telephone box and some flooded quarry workings. Follow the single-track road back to the ferry. If you're thirsty on the way, stop for a drink from the spring at Tobar nan Camacach where a cup is chained to the rock for your use.

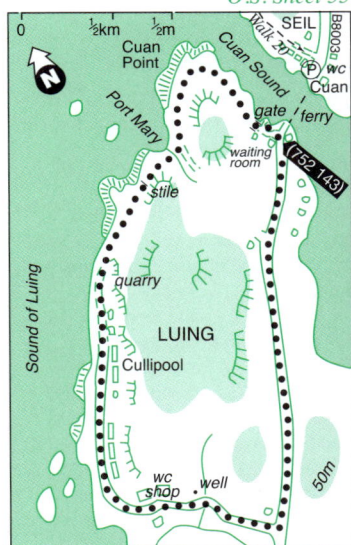

O.S. Sheet 55

Luing Ferry

22 Bonawe Furnace & The River Awe _____ B

A linear walk starting at the mouth of the River Awe, passing an 18th-century iron furnace (well worth a visit), then crossing the river on a dramatic suspension bridge to reach Inverawe Smokehouse. Length: **3½ miles/5.5km** (*there and back*); *Height Climbed:* negligible.

O.S. Sheet 50

Taynuilt is about 11 miles east of Oban on the A85 Glasgow road. Turn into the village and follow the signs for Bonawe Iron Furnace. Follow the road to the shore and park by one of the two piers.

Walk back up the road and, just beyond the first pier, turn left at the sign for Bonawe Iron Furnace. Follow the track passing to the left of the furnace. Go through a gate and keep straight on at the junction of tracks beyond. In a few paces you reach a T-junction at a row of cottages. Turn left here and follow the track through trees.

The track leaves the trees and, level with Inverawe House (across the river to your left), ends at three gates. Go through the gate ahead of you, then turn left, downhill, to reach a bridge over the river (this section can be wet). Cross the bridge, remembering to close the gates at each end – and don't walk in step or you can start alarming oscillations!

Turn left and follow the river bank. After about 500m you are forced right, away from the river, to reach a gate onto the single-track road. Turn right and follow the road (careful of traffic) to reach the entrance to Inverawe Smokery. There is a café, shop and exhibition here, and a short nature trail if you

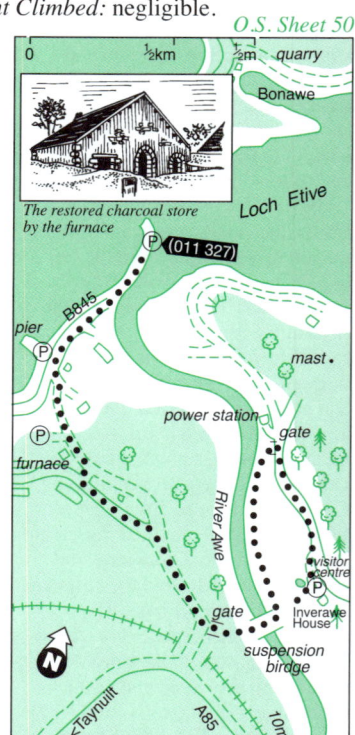

The restored charcoal store by the furnace

wish to extend your walk.

To return to the bridge, follow the signs from the car park for Hugo's Lochan and the Riverside Path past a trout pond, through a kissing gate then over a field.

Retrace your steps to the start.

23 Ben Cruachan _____ A+

The great bulk of Ben Cruachan, its summit the highest point of a seven-summit ridge, dominates north Argyll. This is a steep, rough ascent, but well worth the effort. Length: **7 miles/11km** *(there and back); Height Climbed:* **3600ft/110m**. ***NB: The scrambled section by the summit should not be attempted without previous experience.***

O.S. Sheet 50

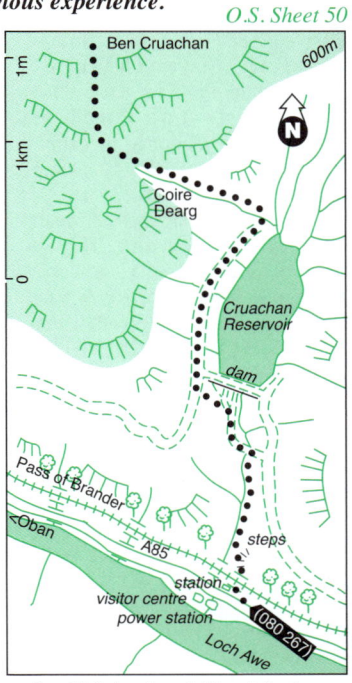

Ben Cruachan is the highest mountain in this area. Its distinctive cluster of peaks, rising to 3689ft/1126m, is one of the region's most visible landmarks, and 'Cruachan' was the war cry of the Campbell clan. More recently a 300ft/100m long cavern was excavated in the mountain to house hydro-electric generators.

To climb the mountain, start about 15 miles east of Oban on the A85 Glasgow road, near the Power Station visitor centre (worth a visit itself). 500m past the visitor centre there is a sign for pedestrian access to the railway station and room to park on the verge beyond. If this is full, there is a lay-by just along the road (pavement on far side).

Follow the sign for the station, but go through a gate and under the railway line (watch your head). Walk up steps beyond the railway and bear left on a clear path which leaves the steps opposite a fenced area. Follow the path as it rises steeply, through trees at first and then onto the grassy hillside, until you join the surfaced road climbing to the Cruachan dam. Turn left along the road. Shortly before you reach the dam head off to the left then, almost immediately, left again on a faint path which leads uphill to join the track that runs along the west side of the reservoir.

Follow this track to its end, then take the rough path up Coire Dearg onto the ridge. Turn right for a rocky scramble to the summit. Descend the same way.

24 Glen Nant Oakwoods _____ C

This is a short, well-marked circular walk through a fine hardwood forest, with some spectacular views of Ben Cruachan. Combine your walk with a visit to the Bonawe Iron Furnace at Taynuilt (Walk 22). These woods provided some of the charcoal for the foundry. Length: **2 miles/3.3km**; *Height Climbed:* **200ft/60m**.

O.S. Sheet 50

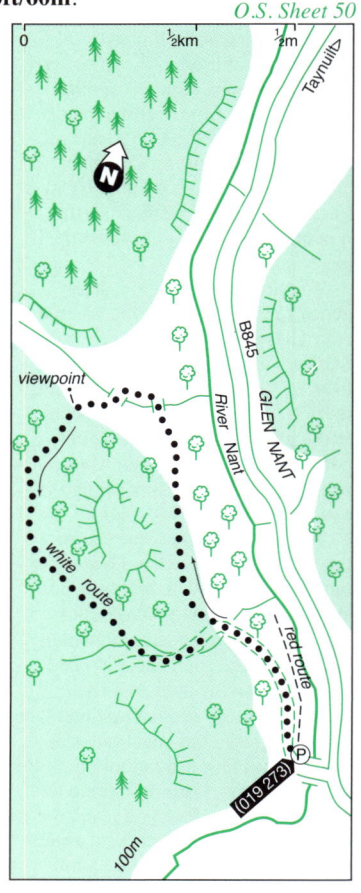

Take the A85 Glasgow road from Oban as far as Taynuilt then turn right onto the B845 for Kilchrenan. Just over 2 miles from Taynuilt turn into a Forestry Commission car park to the right of the road – Glen Nant National Nature Reserve.

There are two signposted routes leaving from the car park. The red route (Riverbank Trail) is a short, all abilities walk along the River Nant. For this walk, however, follow the white route (Ant Trail), which climbs up through the mixed woodland above the river.

The woodland is predominantly oak, a remnant of the native forest whose survival is due largely to the role it played in supplying charcoal to fuel the Bonawe Iron Furnace, built at Taynuilt in 1753 (*see* Walk 22). A steady supply of hardwood was needed to produce charcoal by controlled slow-burning on 'charcoal hearths', and the woods were managed to supply the demand. There are still many sites of old charcoal hearths visible in this and other woods in the area. Information points describing the charcoal-burning industry, and the woodland's abundant animal and insect life, are placed around the walk.

25 Kilchurn Castle   C

A very short there-and-back walk, on a good path, to one of the area's most romantic ruins: an old Campbell stronghold on a promontory jutting out into Loch Awe. Length: **1 mile/1.6km** (there and back); *Height Climbed:* none.

O.S. Sheet 50

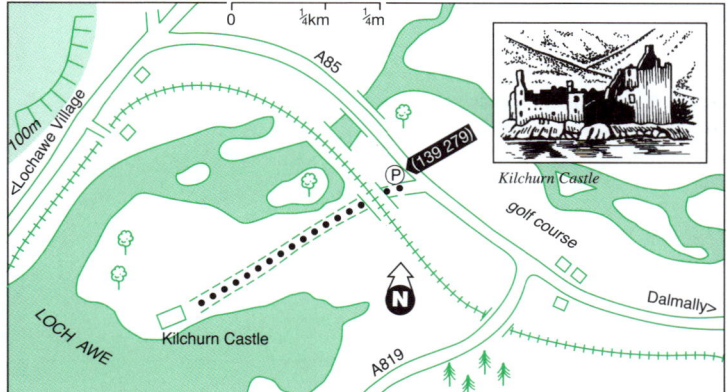

Kilchurn Castle

A little over 20 miles east of Oban, following the A85 Glasgow road, you run along the north shore of Loch Awe, pass through the little village of Lochawe, then turn right, around the end of the loch. The road crosses the River Orchy. Watch for an unsignposted entrance to your right, just beyond, and turn in there. This is the car park for Kilchurn.

The route could not be easier: a path starts from the end of the car park, runs under the railway bridge over the river, then continues along a low, marshy peninsula to reach the castle, visible ahead.

The original castle was built around 1440 by Sir Colin Campbell of Glenorchy – progenitor of the family of the Earls of Breadalbane – with subsequent additions until the late 17th century. By the late 18th century the building was a ruin, by which time the Campbells had long since moved their main seat to Loch Tay. When it was built, the castle would have been on an island; in the early 1800s the water level of the loch was dropped, attaching the island to the shore.

The remaining walls are substantial, and well maintained by Historic Environment Scotland, and there is a fine view down the loch and of the surrounding hills.

Return by the same route.

26 Two Forest Walks _____C

Two groups of waymarked walks through equally interesting but differing woodland, managed by the Forestry Commission.

A Strone Hill _____

Two short walks on good paths through beautiful oak woodland alongside the River Lochy. Picnic benches. Length: **1/2 mile/1km** *(red route);* **1 mile/1.7km** *(green route).* Strone Hill is signposted 3 miles east of Dalmally on the A85. Both paths start from the car park, pass through fine oak woods and include a stretch along the River Lochy. There is a fine view of a waterfall from a short detour off the red route.

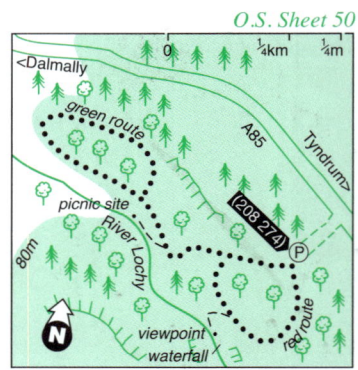

O.S. Sheet 50

B Sutherland's Grove _____

Three walks through mixed woodland. Length: up to **2 miles/3km**. Drive north from Benderloch on the A828. Sutherland's Grove car park is signposted to the right of the road after 4 miles.

The grove is named after Sir John Donald Sutherland, former Commissioner of the Forestry Commission, and contains fine large Douglas Firs.

A short all-abilities route goes west from the car park. The longer red and blue circuits start by the notice board, the latter crossing the burn at a spectacular gorge.

It is possible to follow forest roads up to Glen Dubh reservoir or to extend your walk in either direction along the cycle track (*see* map).

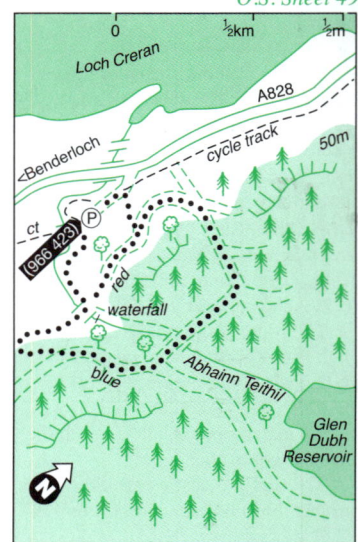

O.S. Sheet 49